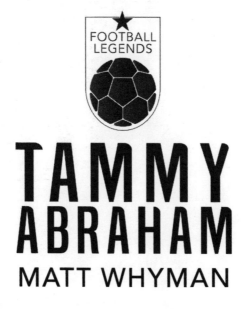

TAMMY ABRAHAM

MATT WHYMAN

T0326013

FOOTBALL LEGENDS

TAMMY ABRAHAM

SCHOLASTIC

Published in the UK by Scholastic Children's Books, 2021
Euston House, 24 Eversholt Street, London, NW1 1DB
A division of Scholastic Limited

London ~ New York ~ Toronto ~ Sydney ~ Auckland
Mexico City ~ New Delhi ~ Hong Kong

SCHOLASTIC and associated logos are trademarks and/or
registered trademarks of Scholastic Inc.

Text © Matt Whyman, 2021
Cover illustration © Stanley Chow, 2021

The right of Matt Whyman to be identified as the author
of this work has been asserted by him in accordance with
the Copyright, Designs and Patents Act, 1988.

ISBN 978 1407 19856 9

A CIP catalogue record for this book
is available from the British Library.

Printed and bound by CPI Group (UK) Ltd, Croydon, CR0 4YY
Papers used by Scholastic Children's Books are made
from wood grown in sustainable forests.

2 4 6 8 10 9 7 5 3 1

While this book is based on real characters and actual historical events,
some situations and people are fictional, created by the author.

UNAUTHORIZED: this book is not sponsored,
approved or endorsed by any person who appears in this book.

www.scholastic.co.uk

Contents

DREAM BIG

It's the closing minutes of a golden game for England. The national side is up an impressive 6–0 against Montenegro at Wembley Stadium. In this Euro 2020 qualifying match, manager Gareth Southgate's young team have dominated the game. They've shown strength, flair and skill, and they've put the ball in the back of the net so many times the win is pretty much guaranteed.

Montenegro might be on the ropes, but one player who has everything to play for is the England striker Tammy Abraham. Fresh on the pitch, having come on as a substitute early in the second half, Tammy brings his trademark energy to the game. A rising star at Chelsea, popular with the fans and a top goalscorer in the 2019–2020 Premiership season, this is still only Tammy's fourth appearance for his country at senior level. While his teammates are beginning to relax, certain they've made it to the final tournament, Tammy is determined to make his mark.

Earlier, Tammy was watching from the bench as the goals flowed. Alex Oxlade-Chamberlain fired in the first goal just ten minutes into the game. Marcus Rashford also joined him on the scoresheet, along with a chaotic own goal by England's opponents. But throughout the game, it was Harry Kane who proved deadly in the box. After he delivered a masterful hat-trick for his country, manager Southgate decided it was time to rest his captain. Trading places with Kane, Tammy joined the game knowing he had some big boots to fill.

In a match that England dominated, Tammy found himself as a centre forward at the heart of the action. He constantly probed the defence for weaknesses, looking to catch them off guard. Tammy searched for spaces to break through, positioning himself to surge and strike when the opposition least expected it, while working closely with his teammates as they fed the ball towards him. The opposition knew that Tammy was one to watch. He's tall – often towering over other players at 6 ft 3 in – wiry, strong and hungry for the goal.

Out on the left wing, with just six minutes to go before full time, Jadon Sancho took possession of the ball. He made a punchy run to outflank his marker, followed by a fast, low cross into the box. Sancho sensed that Tammy would find a touch before the defender had a chance to clear it. As kids, Tammy and Jadon used to knock a ball around together. The pair were playing on the world stage now, a far cry from the local park where they began their football careers. They'd watched each other grow as players, developing skills through experience and building on that same raw instinct that brought them together as boys.

If anyone knew what pace and finish Tammy can unleash when it matters most, it was Jadon Sancho. Back then, the two football-mad friends never imagined in their wildest dreams that they'd be wearing three lions on their shirts. Now here they were under the floodlights at Wembley Stadium, having followed different paths as players to reach this all-important point.

Stealing a cross to break the Montenegro defence, Jadon provided Tammy with the opportunity he needed. The ball moved so quickly across the box that Tammy was forced to slide in, reaching with his foot and glancing the ball towards the left-side post. The keeper reacted from the centre of his line. His outstretched fingertips brushed the ball, but all he could do was watch helplessly as it dropped into the back of the net.

Goal! The seventh for England in the game, but a very special one for the goalscorer.

Tammy rose from his knees as if lifted by the roar that rang out across the stadium, spreading his arms wide victoriously and turning to celebrate with his old friend. They're in shock, but also grinning broadly. For Tammy and Jadon, friends from the moment they first fell in love with football, this is a moment that young players can only dream about. Working together, they'd taken England to one of their highest-scoring victories in history. As for Tammy, he'd just marked his arrival as an international striker destined for greatness.

TAMMY FINDS HIS FEET

Kevin Oghenetega Tamaraebi Bakumo-Abraham, or Tammy as he is known, was born on 2 October 1997 in Camberwell, South London. His parents, Marian and Anthony, had settled in England from Nigeria. They were delighted by the arrival of a son.

Three years later, they had another boy called Timmy. The two brothers were close. When Tammy first showed an interest in playing with a ball, Timmy quickly followed in his footsteps. Growing up, Tammy loved a kickaround with his little brother and their friends. He'd head out to the park, the street or even his driveway for a chance to play.

Tammy's first passion at primary school wasn't football but drama. A tall boy with a big presence, he was once selected to play the part of a bully who picked on a little kid. While Tammy put on a convincing performance as the bad guy, offstage everyone knew him as the exact opposite. Tammy was a kind, humble and thoughtful lad. He worked hard in class, always keen to do well, but also began to show that he had talent in his two feet. Little did Tammy know that, years later, his childhood adventures would go public. A home video surfaced, shared by Chelsea's assistant head coach, Jody Morris, showing a young Tammy and Timmy demonstrating their impressive street dance moves! The clip delighted fans, showing the schoolboy throwing shapes, and it hints at the kind of agile, nimble and swift-moving player Tammy would become.

As well as playing football whenever he could, Tammy loved to watch the game on television. He followed the dramas played out in the Premiership season, and soon found himself supporting a leading team. Surprisingly, it wasn't Chelsea, just five miles down the road and the football home that would help to make his name. Instead, Tammy got behind another local London side, Arsenal. Tammy explains that he was simply following a family tradition in supporting the Gunners, as Arsenal are known. In particular, he grew up in awe of striker Thierry Henry. Tammy was struck by the Frenchman's ability to take risks with the ball, move quickly on his feet and then score in so many different and creative ways. Without doubt, it was an early influence that would come to shape Tammy's own style of play.

A Player in the Making

Tammy continued to shine in dance and drama at school, but it was football that really saw him dazzle. He used his height to his advantage, often winning the ball in the air, and employing his long legs to turn and outrun his opponents.

Each summer, he and up to fifty friends would gather in the park. They'd divide into teams and stage their own competition. It's here that Tammy and Jadon became firm friends.

While the football games could sometimes be scrappy, they often played in small spaces like basketball courts. With little room to stretch out, the pair began to sharpen their skills and one-touch moves. Unusually, for the kind of slender player built to wrap himself around an awkward ball and convert it into a goal, Tammy chose to play back in defence. Here he made up for his slight frame with energy and commitment.

Tammy's enthusiasm marked him out from his fellow players, earning him attention from parents and other spectators. When it came to winning the ball and working as an essential member of his side, everyone could see that Tammy gave it one hundred per cent.

Early Break

With a competitive spirit when it came to football, and hunger to improve, it was only a matter of time before Tammy came to the attention of a scout for Chelsea FC's Under-8s squad, part of the club's famed academy programme, which aims to support young talent and provide coaching and experience to help players reach a professional standard.

An hour by road from his home in Camberwell,

Tammy would have to rely heavily on his parents to drive him to the academy sessions each week. Then there were the youth fixtures that took place on most weekends. It would be a big sacrifice for his mum and dad to make, but also a reflection of how much they believed in their oldest son's potential on the pitch.

For Tammy, joining the academy at Chelsea was the chance he'd been waiting for to sharpen his raw skills. There he would have the opportunity to train with other promising young players and earn valuable game time as well as insight and advice.

A Drive with Drogba

On his first day at the academy, Tammy passed through the security gates feeling excited and a little overwhelmed to be inside this legendary football village. It was cold outside as he made his way to the training fields. Tammy was looking forward to the session so he could warm up. Just then, he paused to admire a sleek car inside the grounds. It took another moment before he recognized the figure behind the wheel. Tammy's eyes widened. It was

Chelsea's superstar striker, Didier Drogba! Before he could blink, Didier opened the window and asked if he wanted a lift to the grounds. It was only a short journey, but Tammy could not believe his luck. He jumped in, buzzing with excitement, and did his best to stay cool as Drogba drove and chatted with him.

Minutes later, having thanked his new friend for the lift and watched him drive away, Tammy looked around for his teammates. He was desperate to tell them what had just happened, barely able to believe it himself, only to realize he was first to arrive.

As young players progress through each year of Chelsea's Academy system, the challenges grow. It meant Tammy had to become increasingly serious about the sport, but that was never in question. The young South Londoner was determined to make his presence known on the pitch.

Total Commitment

Even as a young boy, Tammy knew that if he was going to achieve his dream of becoming a football star he would have to work hard and remain focused. Tammy made the most of each session at the academy while making sure he continued to work hard at school. He credits his parents with keeping him grounded. At a time when he might have been tempted to throw everything at football, his mum and dad reminded him that a good education was vital to whatever path he chose in life. Tammy took this advice to heart. It left little time for anything else, but he was committed. In fact, he now says that without his parents he wouldn't have made such a success of his life as a professional footballer.

Tammy also found that his experience on the pitch actually helped him in the classroom. Even in the youngest squad under the Chelsea Academy scheme, players are taught the importance of a positive mindset. Together with his teammates, Tammy was encouraged to keep working at getting better, as well as experiment and even make mistakes as a means of learning. From an early age, this helped Tammy constantly strive to improve his game as well as his school grades.

Academy Entry

Chelsea FC Academy is part of the club's training centre and grounds, which is situated just outside London in leafy Cobham, Surrey.

Chelsea Academy aims to coach young players with potential, offering support and guidance as they develop. It focuses on young players aged from eight to twenty-three, with teams for different age groups. Most academy students are scouted, which means they are spotted playing for local or school teams by coaches who think the club might be interested in developing them.

Once a scout has spotted a player they think the club might be interested in, they make a recommendation and then the academy coaches might invite that player to a trial. At the trials, coaches look for players that can fill gaps in their current line-up, as well as someone with a strong technique and a personality that will fit in with the team.

ACADEMY AMBITION

Positioned to Strike

Under the guidance of the academy coaches, Tammy's first big change saw him move out from his early favoured position as centre back. While he used his height to play as a defender, taking possession of the ball in the air before his opponents could reach for it, Tammy was often drawn forward into the midfield action. At first, it was suggested to Tammy that he try out on the wings, on both the left and right. There, he could still use his height to his advantage but also put his speed to good use in delivering the ball up the pitch and then feed it to the frontline players.

The switch to the flanks certainly helped Tammy make greater use of his pace, and yet he still had more to give. He would often follow the ball into the centre box, or find a space up front and catch the opposition by surprise. Tammy's hunger for goals did not go unnoticed. Eventually, a coach suggested that he make the move into an attacking position, which is where Tammy found his feet.

Leading the Charge

Having advanced from the back of the formation to the front, Tammy now led the charge with a deep appreciation of defence, midfield and wing positions. With this insight into team play, and his aim now set on scoring, the young striker soon began to show that he had made a smart move. At last, he was in the right place to score. Tammy wasn't a player who loitered in the goalmouth, waiting for the ball, but worked hard with his teammates to create opportunities. Quick on his feet, and regularly leaving the defence in a spin, he soon began to build a reputation as a centre forward that keepers feared.

A Road Away

Even in training, Tammy was known as a player who liked to celebrate goals with his teammates. It reflected his determination on the pitch, and demonstrated to the academy coaches that Tammy understood hard work and commitment would bring results.

Tammy didn't need to be reminded what rewards such dedication might bring one day. Just across the road from the academy grounds in Cobham, Chelsea's first team could often be seen in training. Every young player shared the same dream of graduating into the senior squad. As the coaches often said, it was "only a road away". For a focused young player like Tammy, this was all he needed to keep striving to be the best, and make sure he played football with both heart and soul.

Sometimes, John Terry, England player and Chelsea's captain at the time, would cross over to watch Tammy and his teammates. Tammy was in awe of the great man. He was also aware of the fact that training at the academy was no guarantee for any young player that they would one day join the first team. In fact, so few graduates made it into the squad that some said joining the academy programme was a curse! Tammy simply blocked out such talk. He believed that his generation would be the first to truly break through.

Making the Grade

Unlike many young players at the academy, Tammy chose not to enrol in the full-time programme until he turned sixteen. Instead, having moved from primary to secondary school in Pimlico, Central London, he continued life as an ordinary schoolboy while travelling to Cobham for training twice a week. With a match most weekends, as well as homework to be done, Tammy found he had little time for anything else, but it suited him just fine. While he wasn't playing football as much as some of the boys at the academy, life at home with his family, and at school with his friends, kept him

17

grounded and free from distractions. "I was getting a good balance," he says about his time as a pupil and player. "I knew I had to get my grades so I could focus on football."

RISING THROUGH THE RANKS

Everyone at Chelsea's training grounds knew that Tammy had grown up as an Arsenal supporter. It was a local London team for him, after all. Tammy claims it was no big deal and just fed the banter among his young teammates. In fact, when it came to committing full time to the academy in 2004, he turned down interest from the Gunners' own youth programme to stay at the club that had backed him since he was a little boy. There was no doubt that Tammy felt honoured to have been approached by the team, but in turning it down his commitment to Chelsea was clear for all to see.

Tammy the Academy Ace

Tammy had played with many of his academy teammates from an early age. Once he joined the full-time programme, Cobham seemed like a second home to him. As a result, he swiftly found his place in Chelsea's youth teams.

Having made his debut for the Under-16s in the first match of the 2013–14 season, Tammy's performance saw him switch up to the Under-18s side against West Ham just one week later. Not only that, he scored his first goal for the side in a 2–1 victory for Chelsea.

That season, Tammy scored five times in seventeen appearances for the side, along with many more goals in games with the younger age groups. Even among talented teammates, it made him one to watch.

Unfortunately, a thigh injury prevented Tammy from playing the final games of the season. Having made a full recovery over the summer break, he returned for the 2014–15 fixtures with experience under his belt and fitness on his side. This time, Tammy scored nineteen goals before the Christmas break, securing his reputation as a near unstoppable striker. It was enough for Tammy to return in the New Year with a promotion to the Under-21 squad. Facing many older players proved challenging, but Tammy rose above it. Quick on his feet, and regularly leaving the defence in a spin, he soon began to build a reputation as a centre forward that keepers feared.

Shootout with Solanke

Towards the end of the 2014–15 season, Tammy had scored so often for his Under-21 side that he was a contender for the Golden Boot Award, earned by the player with the most goals. It's an incredible honour at any level. With just one match to go, Tammy found himself one goal behind the leading scorer and fellow Chelsea striker Dominic Solanke.

Going into the final game against Norwich, Tammy was desperate to equal Dominic's tally. As the referee blew the whistle to kick off the match, he only had eyes on scoring. The rivalry between the two players was intense but good humoured, and when Tammy struck the ball into the net, earning him the goal he craved, Dominic Solanke was one of the first to congratulate him.

The pair of star strikers both claimed forty goals that season, so Tammy and Dominic shared the Golden Boot, as well as the memory of a mighty season playing together as Chelsea teammates.

The Young Lion

As well as his club success during his time at the academy, Tammy was thrilled to be called up to the England youth squad. Towards the end of 2014, he made his debut for the Under-18 national side in a match away to Italy. While the Young Lions lost, Tammy only had to wait until the following March when he scored his first international goal in a 6–1 win against Switzerland.

One year later, in the summer of 2016, under the watchful eye of youth team boss Aidy Boothroyd, Tammy helped to steer the Under-19 squad to the semi-final of the European finals in Germany. For the young South Londoner, this chance to make a difference at an international level only strengthened his reputation at the academy as a player who made goals happen.

During his time as a Chelsea youth team player, winning the FA Youth Cup as well as the UEFA Europa League in both 2015 and 2016, Tammy scored a mighty seventy-four goals in ninety-eight matches. What's more, when Dominic Solanke left to join Dutch team Vitesse Arnhem, Tammy found himself in the spotlight as a senior academy striker. With his time as a youth team player drawing to a close, and an impressive record to his name, it was only a matter of time before Tammy received the call-up he'd been dreaming about.

First Team Dream

In October 2015, Tammy committed himself to a future with Chelsea by signing a new contract. He continued to impress on the field, until one day the following spring he learned that he had been picked to train with the first team. His selection was made by Chelsea boss Guus Hiddink. Guus had taken over to cover the departure of José Mourinho, and was impressed by the young striker's performance at the academy. By May 2016, after Tammy showed that he could also make his mark among Chelsea's senior squad, Hiddink offered him a debut place in the line-up as a substitute against Liverpool. Tammy was overjoyed.

In the seventy-fourth minute of the game away at Anfield, Tammy joined the action to replace Bertrand Traoré. While the match ended in a 1–1 draw, Tammy's first taste of Premiership football left him hungry for more.

The following week, in his first appearance at Chelsea's Stamford Bridge home, he traded places with Traoré once more in a match against that season's Premier League winners, Leicester. Despite only appearing on the pitch for a short time again, and with another 1–1 draw, Tammy's performance marked him out as a young player with a promising future. He had talent, enthusiasm and determination on his side. He was liked by teammates and fans, and had a formidable record in youth teams for goalscoring. What Tammy needed, as did any young player starting a professional career, was experience on the field at a senior level.

England Football League System

England's football system is split up into tiers of interconnected leagues. The top three tiers are:

The Premier League
Teams: Twenty
Relegation: The bottom three teams are relegated to the Championship league at the end of the season

English Football League Championship
Teams: Twenty-four
Promotion: At the end of the season the top two teams are automatically promoted to the Premier League; the next four compete in play-offs, with the winner gaining the third promotion spot
Relegation: The bottom three teams are relegated to League One

English Football League One

Teams: Twenty-four

Promotion: The top two teams are automatically promoted to the Championship league; the next four compete in play-offs, with the winner gaining the third promotion spot

Relegation: The bottom four teams are relegated to League Two

AMONG CHAMPIONS

The summer of 2016 sparked a whirlwind of activity for Tammy Abraham. Soon after his maiden game at Stamford Bridge, he joined the England team at the UEFA Under-19 Championship in Germany. Playing with grit and determination, the young striker helped take the team to the semi-finals. They put up an impressive fight against a strong Italian side, but eventually went out 2–1. It was disappointing for Tammy and his teammates, of course, but they all recognized the value of time on the pitch at an international level.

An American Dream

Although the team didn't return with the winner's trophy, Tammy's performance persuaded Chelsea bosses to add him to the squad under new manager Antonio Conte, for a pre-season tour of the United States. Tammy had only just flown back to England when he was off again for a transatlantic trip to America. There, Chelsea took part in International Champions Cup games against formidable opponents such as Real Madrid and AC Milan. From observing each match from the bench to training with the senior squad, Tammy continued to gain vital experience at the highest level of football. It gave him confidence as a player. It also boosted his desire to get as much match time as possible.

At the end of the pre-season tour, Tammy flew back from the States feeling tired but happy. He had enjoyed the opportunity to spend time with the senior team. Now, Tammy turned his attention to the 2016–17 season. With the opening weekend looming, he began to wonder what the club had in store for him.

Switch to City

Often young players join another team on loan. It's a chance for them to gain more playing time, and be a part of a different squad, before returning to their original side as a more mature footballer for the experience. Playing on loan can benefit the player and both teams. Many players on loan feel it's better for their football careers than sitting on the bench waiting for that big break with their main side.

So, when Tammy received a visit at his parents' house from the head coach at Bristol City, shortly after his return from the USA tour, he was happy to listen to what the man had to offer.

The name of the head coach was Lee Johnson. He had been watching Tammy's progress through the academy, and lately with the senior squad. Lee felt that he could offer Tammy an opportunity on loan at City. He had been to see Tammy's coaches at Chelsea, and they were happy for Lee to discuss it with their young striker.

Bristol City were a Championship team, which is the second highest UK football league after the Premiership. Lee explained that the club were looking to take on a promising young player on loan. Impressed by Tammy's achievements at the academy and as a Young Lion, he invited the striker to join The Robins, as Bristol City are known, for the experience. Lee had a vision for Tammy. He set out in great detail the impact he believed Tammy could have on the club and the coming season's championship. Lee told Tammy all about the players at City, and who he would get on with, and described the Ashton Gate stadium where he truly believed that Tammy could make his mark. Tammy liked Lee. He felt that he could trust him, as did Tammy's parents, Marian and Anthony, who had joined in the chat.

By the time Lee Johnson left the Abrahams, Tammy had agreed to join Bristol City on loan. With the 2016–17 season due to start within days, he had little time to pack and say goodbye to his Chelsea teammates. Tammy just hoped that such a move would be the making of his career.

Tammy on Target

Preparing for his first game wearing Bristol City's red shirt, Tammy was well aware that Lee Johnson had taken a risk. He was young, with little experience of senior men's football. Even so, Tammy was determined to prove himself. With The Robins' first game of the season against newly promoted League One champions Wigan Athletic, he started the match on the substitutes' bench and hoped the boss would give him a shot at playing.

Midway through the second half, the two teams level with a goal each, Tammy's moment arrived. With City pressuring the visitors but failing to punch through their defence, Johnson chose to send his new striker onto the pitch to see if he could find a gap. Tammy made his presence known from the first touch. He was keen, as any debut player would be, but the way Tammy skilfully hustled the ball was noticed by both the boss and the fans in the stands. Shortly afterwards, when a corner ball floated into the six-yard box, he used his height to head the ball into the net.

Taking Bristol City 2–1 up, Tammy's touch would

prove to be the winner. His delight was impossible to hide, and coach Lee Johnson knew his instinct to bring the youngster across from Chelsea could transform City's chances of success that season.

The Goal Machine

Halfway through the season, nobody could have predicted what a star turn Tammy would take on loan to Bristol City. His ability to find space in the box and convert the opportunity to goals was soon celebrated by his side and feared by the opposition.

But while Tammy made his mark, The Robins could still struggle against strong competition. In both December and January, the team went without a victory in eight matches. However, it just made Tammy all the more determined to save his new side from relegation. By the end of the 2016–17 season, Bristol City finished seventeenth out of twenty-four teams. As well as surviving in the Championship league, the team recognized that the young player they had signed up on loan had taken the season by storm. Not only had Tammy Abraham scored a stunning twenty-six goals in forty-eight matches,

City's teenage star found himself crowned the Championship's second highest top scorer.

With the season over, it was time for Tammy's loan to Bristol City to come to an end. He left the club as a popular player with staff, fans and his teammates – winning an impressive three club awards as Player of the Year, Top Goalscorer of the Year and Young Player of the Year – along with huge respect and warm wishes for the future from team boss Lee Johnson. In just one season, Tammy had matured as a player, fought hard for every ball, and sealed a loan relationship between Chelsea and Bristol City that thrives to this day.

A SWITCH TO SWANSEA

Life as a professional football player can make it hard to set down roots. Tammy had only just settled into his Bristol apartment and made the city his home when it was time for him to move on.

On loan to The Robins, Tammy had done a lot of growing up. His bosses at Chelsea recognized that the young player had matured with experience. Having signed to keep Tammy for another five years, they hoped to see him grow further by presenting him with an even greater challenge. This time, after seeing their young striker dominate the Championship, Chelsea invited Tammy to see what he could learn from playing in a Premiership side on loan for a season. So, in July 2017, just one day after renewing his contract with Chelsea, Tammy headed out to pick up more playing time with Swansea City.

Struggling Swans

In his first match of the 2017–18 season, playing away to Southampton, Tammy made his debut for a Welsh side that had been struggling in the Premiership. The match ended in a 0–0 draw. It was a flat start to this new chapter in his football career, though his Swansea boss, former Chelsea coach Paul Clement, believed the young striker would soon find his feet. Sure enough, just over a week later Tammy scored his first goal for the team in a 4–1 League Cup win against Milton Keynes Dons.

Both the team and fans alike felt sure that Tammy was set to shine at last, just as he had at Bristol, when he went on to score his first Premier League goal in a 2–0 win against Crystal Palace. Tammy was as committed as ever as the season progressed. Even so, Swansea as a team just could not lock into a winning mode. They struggled through the mid-season, during which Tammy went without a goal until the following February. It was only in an FA fourth round replay with Notts County that he finally broke his goal drought by scoring not once but twice. After their struggles, the team finally tasted success – and did so in style. Tammy assisted in another two goals in the game, which would earn Swansea a stunning 8–1 victory.

Disappointingly, the team were unable to build on this decisive victory through the remaining matches of the season. It was a frustrating experience for Tammy, but he never stopped fighting for his side. He continued to show flashes of brilliance, but critics were quick to point out when Tammy had a loose touch on the ball, which allowed the opposition to steal possession from him. Tammy's supporters and teammates looked upon him with sympathy. They could see that the young striker was making the very best of limited opportunities. Sadly, it would not be enough to save Swansea from relegation to the Championship league.

End of the Road?

As his 2017–18 season came to a close, Tammy began to consider his future as a footballer. He had scored just eight goals in thirty-nine appearances for Swansea. While this might be an impressive scoresheet for some strikers, it did not compare to his performance at Bristol City the previous year and Tammy was disappointed.

As a player on loan, Tammy knew full well that the Chelsea bosses would be watching. As the side he had joined for a season slipped out of the Premiership, Tammy wondered if they would keep faith in him. He knew that he had more potential to unlock. It was just a question of finding a team that could allow the centre forward to turn opportunities with a ball into goals.

Tammy did not have to worry for long. Even though the Swans were relegated that season, his coaches at Chelsea had not lost sight of the fact that the young player could be brilliant on the pitch. While a flat performance from other players on loan might have marked the end of their hopes of a Premiership career, the new Chelsea manager,

Maurizio Sarri, felt that Tammy had more to offer. He believed that under the right circumstances, in a team that supported their young hope and allowed him to thrive, Tammy could prove himself.

Rising to the Challenge

Tammy knew that this would be his last chance. It was likely that he would be given just one more season to show that he had what it takes to earn a place at Chelsea and play at Premiership level. If this failed, his dream could well be over.

Rather than be downcast about the situation, Tammy reminded himself why he loved to play football. He was known for his sheer enthusiasm for the sport, whether he was playing a Premier League fixture or just kicking a ball around in his parents' garden with his younger brother, who was showing promise as a footballer with Charlton Athletic. It made no difference to Tammy. He simply loved to play and had no desire to stop now. Tammy also reflected on how far he'd come, and all the people who had supported him along the way. From his family and friends, coaches and teammates, nobody had ever given up on him. He was also in a steady relationship with his girlfriend, the lifestyle vlogger Leah Monroe, who supported him every step of the way. Tammy owed it to them, as much as himself, to prove that he was good enough to play football with the best in the world.

VILLA THRILLER

Two months into the 2018–19 season, Tammy played his first game on loan with a new team, Aston Villa. It marked a return to the Championship league for the striker, but Tammy didn't see this as a step back. He had arrived in a positive frame of mind. With great memories of his time in the league at Bristol City, his sole focus was on making a difference at Villa.

Fan Favourite

In his debut for the team, Tammy came close to scoring twice in a 1–1 draw against Blackburn Rovers. It would be Villa's fifth Championship game that season without a win. Tammy was determined to turn it around for them. Four days later, half an hour into the game, he scored the first goal in a 2–0 victory over Rotherham United. Having slotted the ball low into the left-hand corner of the net, Tammy faced his team's supporters behind the goal and celebrated with them. Not only did it mark The Villans' first victory in a long time, this was the confidence boost he needed. Now it was just a question of building on it.

The Aston Ace

On 28 November, Tammy silenced any critics who claimed he had lost his form at Swansea. In a thrilling match against Nottingham Forest, the tall and nimble South Londoner scored not one but four goals in an incredible 5–5 draw. It was a result that would make history, with Tammy becoming the first

Villa player in the twenty-first century to score so highly in one game.

This was only the beginning of what would prove to be a winning streak. Four months into the season, Tammy had claimed an incredible fourteen goals. At the start of 2019, with another two balls in the back of the net to his name, Tammy became joint top goalscorer in the Championship league.

For a player on loan, Tammy's scoresheet was remarkable. It also led to talk in the press that Chelsea might now decide it was time to cash in their investment in the young striker and recall him to play for the first team.

At the same time, Tammy's performance in the first half of the season drew attention from other clubs. Even some Premiership sides were keen to sign the striker for his game-changing abilities. Despite it all, Tammy remained committed to Aston Villa for the rest of his loan period. Knowing that Chelsea were fully behind him, he believed The Villans deserved to be promoted to the Premier League.

After his challenging year at Swansea, he was proving himself to be a consistent finisher. Often

42

he would steal a goal as the opposition scrambled to clear the ball from the box, and Villa relied on him to make sure no such opportunity went to waste. His combination of agility and quick wits had finally come together and his performance as a centre forward was impressing both Tammy's critics and fans – people even began to compare Tammy to the legend he had met on his first day at the academy: Didier Drogba.

Pursuit of Promotion

The following April, having scored in a 2–0 victory over Bolton Wanderers, Tammy equalled legendary Villa player Andy Gray's 1997 record of twenty-five goals in one season. By the end of the 2018–19 season, Aston Villa finished fifth in the Championship league. That put them into the play-offs, which saw Tammy score in the semi-final against West Bromwich Albion. Following a 2–1 win against Derby in the final, the team sealed their promotion to the Premiership, and hailed their loan player as a hero.

During his time with Aston Villa, Tammy scored

twenty-six goals in forty appearances. That made him the second highest-scoring player in the league for that season. Everyone could see that Tammy had matured into a first-class professional footballer.

Where Next?

With Tammy hailed by both the club and fans for his role in Villa's promotion campaign, it was no surprise that the club were interested in extending his loan. Under normal circumstances, Tammy might well have signed up for another season. Earlier in 2019, however, football's governing body (FIFA) announced that Chelsea had broken certain transfer rules about buying, selling and swapping youth players on the international market.

In their ruling, FIFA decided that the club had overlooked strict guidelines that protect the welfare of players under the age of eighteen. Chelsea appealed against the ruling, claiming they had broken no such laws. Even so, FIFA banned the club from taking part in that year's spring and summer transfer windows when clubs are allowed to trade.

Unable to take on new footballers, Chelsea were

left to consider only those players who were already signed to the club. Their academy meant they had lots of talented young players, after all. With few opportunities to join the senior team, because most players were signed from international clubs, many like Tammy were playing on transfer elsewhere. Over the years, many critics of Chelsea's Academy claimed this was a failing of the system. They claimed those youngsters enrolled in the academy never stood a chance of playing for the senior side. One positive outcome from the ban on signing new players was that this created an unexpected opportunity for academy students like Tammy. It meant that after his outstanding performance at Villa that season, Tammy found himself under the spotlight at Chelsea as a possible first team striker.

Not only that, Tammy's performance on the pitch that season opened up an opportunity for him to play at a senior level for his country.

ENGLAND'S DREAMING

All through his time on loan, playing for Swansea City, Bristol City and Aston Villa, Tammy had been called up to play for England at youth levels.

Having impressed England youth team boss Aidy Boothroyd at the 2016 UEFA Under-19 Euros, the young striker found himself in the Under-21 team. On his full debut in October 2016, he scored twice in the Euro qualifier against Bosnia and Herzegovina, which England won 5–0. Despite being two years younger than most of his teammates, the result secured a place for Tammy in the team as the England Under-21s went into the 2017 Euro finals in Poland.

When the team reached the semi-finals and found themselves up against a strong German side, Tammy knew they faced a tough challenge. Sure enough, from kick-off the opposition slowly applied pressure to the Young Lions. When Germany went ahead, England did well to equalise just minutes later. As a striker against a side that were increasingly dominating the match, forcing England's defence to work hard, Tammy found his opportunities limited at the other end of the field. Minutes into the second half, however, he struck the ball from a fast cross and put the team ahead. With a place in the final at stake, Germany countered with a goal of their own. Extra time did nothing to change the 2–2 score, which put Tammy on the spot when it came to penalties.

Stronger for the Experience

This was real pressure. After the team had come so far, the shootout would decide whether they ended their Euro campaign in elation or heartbreak. At an international level, Tammy and his teammates were aware that the England senior team had gone out at this stage in both the 1990 World Cup and Euro 96. The hopes of the nation rested on five players, who took turns alongside Germany to see who would go through.

England's first penalty went in, only to be matched by the opposition. Another goal from the England team took them ahead 2–1. Tammy was third in line, giving him the opportunity to score the winning goal. As if that wasn't enough to test his nerves, when Tammy placed the ball on the spot he couldn't help but notice the German keeper, Pollersbeck, pull a scrap of paper from his sock. *What's he doing?* he thought as the keeper unfolded it, and then realized Pollersbeck had made notes about what to expect from the players he faced.

It was enough to unsettle Tammy as he prepared to take the shot. Would the keeper know what he had in mind, or should he place the ball in an unexpected way? As the stadium fell quiet, all Tammy could do was struggle to keep cool and strike the ball. It was a fine effort, but stopped by the keeper, placing both teams on 2–2 draw after three penalties each.

Missing a penalty is a nightmare feared by every player. With just one chance for them to score, anything can go wrong. Walking away from the penalty spot, his strike saved, Tammy could barely believe what had just happened. With his role in the game over, all he could do was watch as his next two teammates took their shots in an attempt to keep England in the game. Unfortunately, Nathan Redmond followed in Tammy's footsteps and failed to score. When Germany planted their final penalty in the net, and the German fans erupted in joy, Tammy and his teammates were left feeling both exhausted and defeated. Aidy Boothroyd had to remind them all that losing is a learning experience. Ultimately, once they had come to terms with the loss, it could make them stronger.

For Tammy, playing in the 2017 Under-21 Euros earned him plenty of praise as a lone striker. Even so, he was still stinging from that missed penalty. Tammy had allowed the keeper to mess with his concentration, but he refused to let that happen again. With the coach's advice in mind, he worked hard on staying focused under pressure. It meant that if he ever faced a similar situation again, he would be ready.

Tournament Test

In 2018, Tammy was disappointed not to join the senior England squad as they travelled to Russia for the FIFA World Cup. He was among many talented young hopefuls left at home, but felt sure his time would come. Tammy was reminded of this when he was selected to play for England's Under-20 side in the Toulon Tournament that year. A competition hosted in France, featuring young national sides from across the globe, this was Tammy's taste of World Cup football, and he set out to make his mark.

England were drawn in a group with Mexico, China and Qatar. As the cup holders from the previous two years, the team set out as the defending champions with an opening match against China. With both teams level at 1–1, it was Tammy who delighted in slotting home the winning goal. While coach Aidy Boothroyd decided to rest the young striker for the next match against Mexico, he returned to the final group match against Qatar and scored in a powerful 4–0 win.

England were drawn against Scotland in the semi-finals, which they won 3–0, before facing

Mexico in the final. With a chance to win for a third year running, the team seemed tense in the early stages of the game. With their opponents stealing a goal in the opening minutes, it looked like the pressure might have got to the young England side. After his penalty disappointment in the Under-21 Euros, however, Tammy was determined to stay cool. With their young striker leading the charge, the team pushed back to finish the first half 2–1 up. In the second half, with everything to play for, Tammy rattled the side post with a thunderous shot. He could not have come closer to scoring, and this show of strength clearly rattled the opposition. By now, England had victory in their sights and celebrated with the trophy at the final whistle.

For the Under-21 players who had led England to victory for the third year running, they knew that the senior team bosses would be watching back home. For Tammy, the dream of playing for his country burned brighter than ever before. In a bid to be selected, he knew that all he could do was keep playing football to the very best of his abilities.

A CHANCE AT CHELSEA

Let's be Frank

Chelsea's 2019–20 campaign in the Premiership was led by a new team boss. Former Chelsea player Frank Lampard became the team's first English manager in over twenty years. Already a legend at the club, Frank held the record as their all-time leading goalscorer.

Tammy's childhood footballing hero would be the one to give the young striker the break he needed in a blue shirt. He had grown up watching Frank play, and even serve as captain through much of one season. Through Tammy's eyes, the former midfielder had real leadership qualities. Frank was also passionate about giving young players a chance, and so Tammy felt sure that he could shine under his guidance. When Frank appointed former academy coach Jody Morris to be his assistant, it really did seem as if a youth revolution was about to happen at the club. With the transfer ban in place, and all eyes on possible call-ups from the academy, all Tammy could do was hold his breath.

When the call came through confirming that his time had come, just as his loan period at Aston Villa ended, Tammy could barely contain his joy. He was determined to show everyone that his new boss had made the right choice.

The Number Nine Curse

On his return to Chelsea, excited about playing for the senior team at last, Tammy was given the number nine shirt. It was a thrill to see his name on the back, but Tammy was aware that the number nine had a particular history at the club. People often said that players who took on the number struggled to shine. Unwilling to let anything get in the way of this opportunity, Tammy wrote off the story as 'rubbish'. Instead, he considered it to be an honour to wear the same number as football stars from the past such as Jimmy Floyd Hasselbaink and Fernando Torres. There was no way he would let superstition get the better of him. Instead, he set out to prove that what mattered most was his performance on the pitch.

Testing Times

With a new coach, Chelsea faced Manchester United in their first competitive match of the 2019–20 Premier League season. With the transfer ban in place, and following the departure of star player Eden Hazard to Real Madrid, Frank fielded a strikingly young side. Four of the players who started the game had come up through the academy system. On the pitch at kick-off, Tammy took his position alongside Mason Mount, Andreas Christensen and Fikayo Tomori. It was a daring move by Frank, but the ban left him with little choice. Even so, Frank was determined to prove it was the best move for the team. Like the others, Tammy felt the weight of responsibility as the referee started the match. He also just wanted to get out and play his very best football.

Four minutes into the game, Tammy came within an inch of becoming the first on the scoresheet. Just inside the eighteen-yard box, the young striker turned with the ball as it came to him and struck it towards the far side of the goal. The ball hit the post, much to the dismay of the team and their fans who had travelled to Old Trafford to watch the match. If Tammy hoped this was an early sign of strength, he was soon to be disappointed. Even though Chelsea played a strong game, they also made a string of mistakes to finish 4–0 down to the home side. It was the team's biggest defeat for a new manager in over forty years. Unsurprisingly, the result focused attention on the younger members of the new line-up, and in the post-match interview Frank faced questions about whether the academy graduates were cut out to play at Premiership level. Naturally, he defended his choice and stressed that he believed they would all come through.

Listening to the interview, Tammy knew what was expected of him.

The Premier League Competition Format

The football season runs from August to May. Throughout the season, each club plays every other Premier League club twice – once at their opponents' stadium and once at their home stadium – for a total of thirty-eight games. The team's ranking is based on their total points, then goal difference and then goals scored. The points are awarded as follows:

Win: three points
Draw: one point
Loss: no points

Shootout Shocker

In Chelsea's next competitive match, Tammy was included in a line-up that included more mature players. In Frank's view, it was just a question of finding the right balance between experience and the talented youth he had called up to the frontline. It was an important game in the UEFA Super Cup, with Chelsea taking on Liverpool in Istanbul. The two teams had a history of playing tight matches against each other, and this was no exception. While Chelsea's performance improved from the previous game, and with many claiming the team were the better side on the night, it would become one of Tammy's most testing moments in his career to date.

Drawing level at 2–2 after extra time, both teams faced a penalty shootout. It was a tense and nervous affair that kept Liverpool and Chelsea neck and neck to the final shot. As Tammy placed the ball on the penalty spot, he knew that the fate of his team in the Super Cup rested on this final kick. But after his disappointing experience at the Under-21 2017 Euro finals against Germany, he was determined not to let the pressure get to him – if the goalkeeper pulled notes out of his sock, or any other trick to distract him, Tammy would see straight through it. He kept his chin up as he swept in to take the kick, doing everything right as he had taught himself, only to watch in dismay as the keeper saved the ball. Tammy had struck it with poise and direction. It was just pure bad luck.

That evening, Tammy left the stadium with the weight of the world on his shoulders. Missing such a vital penalty, which saw Chelsea knocked out of the Super Cup, would be hard for any player to recover from. For Tammy, this came at a time when critics were questioning whether young players like him deserved a place on the team. All he could do was tune out from it all and listen to his boss.

Despite the loss, Frank had expressed nothing but pride in his players. Even though it stung, Tammy knew that the same fate could happen to anyone from the penalty spot. There were no certain goals when it came to taking penalties. What mattered, Frank told him, was that he'd shown the confidence to step up in the first place. That mattered more than the outcome. Even so, it was a tough experience, and Tammy had to dig deep to remind himself that it could make him stronger.

TESTING TIMES

As a young player, new to the senior team, Tammy's performance against Liverpool opened him up to a new level of criticism. He took responsibility for the missed penalty. Even so, many people still pointed out that earlier in the game he had made a controversial appeal for a handball in a tussle with the Liverpool keeper. The referee had awarded Chelsea a penalty, much to the dismay of the Liverpool fans, who felt it wasn't deserved. So it was with some glee that they watched Tammy fail to score in the shootout.

Standing up to Racism

Disturbingly, as well as the jokes and banter after the match, Tammy was also the target of racist abuse. It happened soon after the final whistle. In the dressing room, Tammy checked out social media to see how people were reacting to the game. What he read from a very small minority was both completely unacceptable and deeply troubling. Tammy reported it immediately to the Chelsea bosses, but his main concern was for his family. In particular, he worried about how his mum would handle it. "She was in tears," he told a reporter from CNN. "For me. I'm always a strong character. It doesn't affect me as much. But it could affect people who don't have my personality."

By speaking up, Tammy found himself surrounded by support from his club, teammates, fans, friends and family. In a post-match press conference Frank expressed his disgust at the incident. He stressed that it did not represent the club's spirit, and that he had nothing but admiration for Tammy's conduct both on the pitch and off it. Frank revealed that in fact his young striker had volunteered to take the final penalty. Tammy was aware of the pressure, he said, but wanted to show bravery at a game where the world was watching. Even though it ended in disappointment, Frank was determined that a few small-minded people wouldn't take away from Tammy's winning attitude. Above all, Frank praised Tammy for standing up to racism by speaking out and encouraged other players to follow his example.

For Tammy, Frank Lampard's support through this testing time meant so much to him. It gave him the confidence to move on from the experience knowing that discrimination of any kind had no place in football. It also allowed him to focus on the next match, and prove he had earned his place in the first team squad.

A Turn in Fortune

One week after the Super Cup loss, following a 1–1 draw against Leicester in the Premiership, Chelsea's third match of the season took them away to Norwich. There, on 24 August 2019, just four minutes into the game, Tammy scored his first goal for the Chelsea senior team. With the ball floating in from the right, he found a gap in the defence wall and smashed the ball home. After experiencing disappointment in the penalty shootout against Liverpool, this was a moment he could savour. It was a class goal and the first glimpse for many fans of the reason why Frank Lampard had given the young striker a chance in the squad. Norwich came back to equalise, before another former academy graduate, Mason Mount, took Chelsea ahead once more. When Norwich put another ball away to bring the score level at 2–2, it looked like both teams would have to settle for a draw in a hard-fought game.

With time ticking, Chelsea midfielder Mateo Kovačić played a long ball to Tammy and caught the opposition on the back foot. Tammy responded by taking on the remaining two defenders. In a stunning move, showing focus, quick thinking, bravery and skill, he then weaved around them both before shooting the ball with a decisive right foot past the keeper. As the Chelsea stands erupted in what would finish with a 3–2 victory for Chelsea, Tammy found himself surrounded by his thrilled teammates.

At last, The Blues were living up to the promise

Frank Lampard had made to fans at the start of the season. A young generation of homegrown players like Tammy Abraham, as well as his fellow graduates from the academy such as Mason Mount and Fikayo Tomori, really could work alongside the more mature players to create a winning team. It had just been a question of allowing the team to settle together, and for the academy graduates to build their confidence and find their feet.

As a leading team in the Premiership, Chelsea's nightmare with the transfer ban had transformed into a dream ticket for talented young players like Tammy. For years, critics had said that those who worked their way through the academy system stood little chance of making it to the first team. There was just no room as the club traded on the international market for world-class players. Now, Tammy and several of his teammates who had also graduated from the academy were proving that it was possible. Just as Tammy had idolized Chelsea legends like Didier Drogba, youngsters new to the academy were looking at Tammy and hoping they could follow in his footsteps.

Scoring Spree

One week later, Tammy followed up his Norwich success by scoring both goals in a 2–0 victory over Sheffield United.

With the match played at Chelsea's Stamford Bridge stadium, this was Tammy's first taste of scoring for the senior team in front of a home crowd. In his next game against Wolverhampton Wanderers, which they won 5–2, he became Chelsea's youngest ever player to score a hat-trick. When it came to good-natured banter, many teased Tammy for the fact that he was also responsible for an own goal in the game. They joked that he must have felt bad for the opposition after his treble that he decided to score one for them. Even so, they recognized that their young striker was a remarkable talent with the potential for a dazzling career. A delighted Frank Lampard even suggested that if Tammy continued to play at this level then he might earn himself a place in the England squad.

All of a sudden, having notched up seven goals in just three games, Tammy found himself at the top of the Premiership's scoring charts. His strike rate continued into November of that year, as did Chelsea's winning streak. With five league victories in a row, Tammy helped take the team to six with a goal in their 2–0 victory against Crystal Palace. As the ball rifled into the back of the net, Tammy became Chelsea's second-youngest player to score ten goals in one Premiership season. Fans and commentators began to talk about him in the same breath as stars like Leicester's Jamie Vardy, and as a possible understudy to England's star striker, Harry Kane.

Despite the attention, Tammy was well aware that the 2019–20 season had a long way to go. The young striker knew that if he wanted to live up to the hype then he would have to keep scoring at the same impressive rate. He was playing at the highest level now. It was just a question of keeping it consistent.

THREE LIONS AT LAST

The Nigeria Question

Tammy Abraham has always been proud of his Nigerian heritage. He has spent his whole life in England, and yet his parents' roots are an important part of his identity. It meant that while he grew up dreaming of playing for England, he was also eligible to represent the birthplace of his mother and father.

Competition for a place on any national side is intense. Back in 2015, Tammy was delighted to be called up by England to play for the Under-18 team. He went on to represent his country at both Under-19 and Under-21 level, but what he dreamed of more than anything was a place on the senior team.

In 2017, Tammy was shining brightly on loan to Bristol. His reputation as a goalscorer wasn't just attracting attention in the Premiership but around the world. In September of that year, he found himself faced with an invitation that would require serious consideration. The president of Nigeria's Football Federation, Amaju Pinnick, was reported as saying that Tammy would be playing for the national side. On the same day, Tammy issued a statement to correct the claim and confirm that he still wished to be considered for selection by England.

Two months later, with attention on Tammy's international future in focus, he received the call-up he had wished for all this time. Representing England meant that there was no further chance he could play for Nigeria. Now it was a question of proving himself to national team bosses.

First Caps

In 2017, Tammy was one of three uncapped players called up to the senior England team for friendlies against Germany and Brazil. Tammy first stepped out with three lions on his shirt in a friendly against Germany at Wembley, which ended 0–0. This was an opportunity for manager Gareth Southgate to try out new players to energize the team after their successful but somewhat flat performance in the qualifiers for the 2018 World Cup.

Tammy joined what was billed as England's most inexperienced side since 1980, along with academy graduate Ruben Loftus-Cheek and goalkeeper Jordan Pickford. Tammy had hoped that if he trained hard he might be included as a substitute, and so it came as a surprise to find he would be starting the game. It was a big step up for them all, but none of the debut England players disappointed.

Tammy was unlucky not to score at one point, seeing his strike on goal deflected by a scrambled German defence. It was a close call, however. Although Tammy could see that the ball wasn't going in, the fans were on their feet. He had never experienced such passion. Tammy hoped that another opportunity would come so he could give them what they wanted.

The game against the 2014 World Cup winners resulted in a draw, but England were praised for their performance. After the match, Gareth Southgate talked up the promise he had seen from the new players on the pitch. Without doubt, it was a work in progress, and a chance for the boss to experiment ahead of the 2020 Euro qualifiers. With the World Cup just under a year away, however, it seemed a stretch to think that he would drastically reshape the team that had qualified to go to Russia. Even so, Tammy had made a good first impression for his country.

On 14 November, Tammy earned his second England cap at Wembley in another friendly. Like the match against Germany, they faced a formidable opposition from Brazil. This time, with Southgate still exploring new pathways for his team, Tammy started on the bench. He replaced Marcus Rashford with just fifteen minutes left before the final whistle. While the match ended in a 0–0 draw, the England side were noted for holding a formidable team at bay that included legends such as Neymar and Filipe Luís. For Tammy, it was a chance to gain more experience at an international level and find the same goalscoring form he showed in domestic matches.

Playing the Long Game

Tammy was disappointed not to be selected for the 2018 FIFA World Cup campaign in Russia. Like many elite English players who also remained at home, such as Jack Wilshere and Joe Hart, he'd had high hopes that Gareth Southgate would include him in the squad. At the same time, Tammy knew that he had been playing his very best football in recent months. He could hold his head up high, and he listened to those who reminded him that he was still young. His time would come. It was just a question of staying focused, gaining more experience and constantly striving to improve as both a striker and a team player.

In the summer of 2018, England reached the semi-finals of the World Cup but ended up losing 2–1 to Croatia after extra time. For players like

Tammy who missed out on selection, it had been tough to sit out the tournament. Like any fan, however, all the players watching from home got behind the team. Soon afterwards, and following his testing season on loan with Swansea City, Tammy joined Aston Villa for the 2018–19 Championship. As the goals began to flow, and the club embraced him as a rising star, football pundits began to talk once more about the young striker as a serious England possibility.

By the time Tammy returned to Chelsea to play for the first team in the 2019–20 Premiership season, his game had clearly matured. There was no question about his ability to score, but his passing had become more certain and precise. There was no doubt that Tammy himself wished to play at a national level, and rumours continued to swirl that Nigeria wished to take him on. It would have been a tempting offer, and many said that Tammy was giving it serious consideration once again. Whether or not it was enough to persuade the England boss to act, in order to claim Tammy first, but in October 2019 he received a call-up for the UEFA Euro 2020 qualifying matches.

In Competition

Having played two friendly matches for England, Tammy made his first competitive but brief appearance on 11 October 2019 against the Czech Republic in Prague.

Tammy started on the bench as England got off to a good start, with Harry Kane slotting home a penalty in the fourth minute following a foul on Raheem Sterling. Even so, the team never quite performed to expectation, and finished the second half level at 1–1. When the Czech Republic went ahead with a late goal, Tammy was warming up on the touchline. He was desperate to get involved, and finally replaced Declan Rice in midfield. Sadly, with just two minutes left in the game, there was nothing he could do to save England from defeat. Instead, by playing competitively in a Three Lions shirt, it put to rest any further talk that he would play for Nigeria. Tammy was now committed to England, and in his next England match that would pay off.

Just over a month later, on 14 November 2019, Tammy was included in the squad for England's Euro group qualifier against Montenegro at

Wembley. This would be the team's one thousandth international match, which made the game feel even more special for the players as they left the dressing room for the pitch.

Goal!

Starting on the bench once again, Tammy hoped this time he would see more of the match. He was well aware that in Harry Kane the England team already had a formidable striker, and this was made apparent in a game that saw England vastly improve on their previous match when Harry scored not one goal but three. With Marcus Rashford and Alex Oxlade-Chamberlain also making the scoresheet, England's place in the 2020 Euro finals was pretty much guaranteed.

In some ways, Harry's incredible hat-trick was key to Tammy experiencing match play. Keen to rest the captain and star striker, boss Gareth Southgate subbed on the Chelsea centre forward shortly after the start of the second half.

Tammy got stuck in from the start. Playing up front, he enjoyed witnessing an own goal from

Montenegro at close range. That was nothing compared to a goal of his own, of course, and it wasn't long before he found his own way on to the scoresheet. In the eighty-fourth minute, a low cross from his old friend Sancho allowed him to slip the ball into the net.

For a young striker used to scoring, this one meant the world to Tammy. With England now a staggering 7–0 up, the game had become a showcase. Even so, Tammy had just shown that he could make a difference at an international level. After a year of waiting, and dreaming of a place on the squad, he had been given a chance and proven himself. As Wembley Stadium erupted, and his teammates flocked around him in celebration, Tammy thought about all the friends and family who had helped him on his journey to this moment.

Even as the final whistle blew and the England players left to celebrate in the dressing room, Tammy hoped this would just be the beginning of his international career.

TRUE BLUE

Learning from Losses

Back in the Premiership, following their match against Crystal Palace in early November 2019 where Tammy scored in a 2–0 victory, Chelsea went on to experience a challenging fortnight.

Like his teammates, Tammy knew the first match away against Manchester City was going to be tough. City are a strong side, and so when Chelsea went ahead with an early goal from N'Golo Kanté the fans went wild. When City came back with two goals in a short space of time, Tammy worked hard up front to respond. In the second half, Frank Lampard called him off and replaced him with Batshuayi. All Tammy could do was watch from the bench, hoping that this switch in strategy would break City's strong defence. Sadly, despite the view that The Blues had pushed at every opportunity, the game ended in a 2–1 defeat.

It was the first game without a win for Frank's side since September, dropping Chelsea to fourth in the Premiership. Afterwards, Frank reminded everyone that their response to the loss could bring them closer as a team. It was a question of learning lessons and moving on stronger for the experience.

Pain in Spain

Frank chose his words wisely, aware that Chelsea would be facing the Spanish side Valencia CF the following week in the Champions League qualifier. Once again, Tammy featured in the starting line-up, and he tested the host team's defences from the outset. Valencia responded with some fierce counter-attacking, with both teams scoring early.

Then, just before the half-time whistle, disaster

struck for Tammy. He'd challenged for a high ball, only to fall awkwardly on his hip. A tense few minutes followed as the medics assessed him on the ground, before deciding to stretcher him from the pitch. Chelsea went on to draw with Valencia 2–2, but Tammy's condition remained a cause for concern. He had appeared to be in great pain on the ground, and fears mounted about the severity of the injury. Having scored twelve goals in the 2019–20 Premiership season for both club and country, Tammy would be greatly missed from the pitch if the injury was severe. To the fans' relief, Tammy appeared in an interview after the match. He explained that he had feared the worst when it happened, but that the pain had eased by the time he made it to the dressing room.

Rest and Return

Despite the positive signs, Frank decided to rest Tammy for the next match against West Ham in the Premiership. It proved to be a surprisingly testing game for Chelsea, who failed to break a strong defence and lost 1–0. With the second Premiership defeat in a row, fans found little to cheer about as they left the stadium. The following week, a reporter asked Tammy whether he would be fit for the next match against Aston Villa. In response, Tammy gave a confident thumbs up. For Chelsea's supporters, it would be a welcome return.

Going into the game against Villa was always going to be difficult for Tammy. He had spent a year on loan with The Villans the previous season, scored twenty-six goals for the club and earned the respect of fans and players alike. At the same time, as a professional player Tammy was determined to represent Chelsea with the same passion and commitment as he would in any other match.

High Praise

Twenty-four minutes into the game, the young striker reminded everyone at the stadium why Aston Villa had wanted to keep him when he headed the ball past the keeper from ten yards. As the Chelsea fans went wild, Tammy kept his head down in respect. There was no hint of glee or celebration from the young striker. He had done his job by scoring, and at the same time recognized that only the season before the opposition had been the making of him.

In the post-match interview, the Aston Villa team boss, Dean Smith, praised Tammy highly. He had wanted to keep him at Villa, but recognized that his future lay with a top-flight team like Chelsea. "I'm really, really pleased for him," Dean said to finish. The fact that he was talking about a player in the squad that had just beaten his team spoke volumes. As a striker and young man passionate about the game, Tammy had earned a reputation in a short space of time as a well-liked player with a bright future ahead of him. Meanwhile, out on the terraces, the Chelsea fans recognized what a special player they had in their midst, and a chant rang out as they left the stadium:

Oh Tammy Tammy, Tammy Tammy Tammy Tammy Abraham!

THE ABRAHAM EFFECT

Riding high in the 2019–20 Premier League table, Chelsea's investment in homegrown young players had begun to pay off at last. Alongside Tammy, Chelsea's first team now featured Callum Hudson-Odoi, Ruben Loftus-Cheek, Mason Mount and Fikayo Tomori.

As well as players he had known since he was eight years old, Tammy and his fellow graduates benefited from the fact that key academy coaching staff like Jody Morris had now been appointed by Frank Lampard to support the senior team. With loan experience under their belts, Tammy and his friends were now playing at elite level with a coaching squad who had shared their journey this far.

Inspirational Abraham

"It's the best time for me to be at Chelsea," Tammy told a reporter as they looked back at his 2019–20 season so far. He then credited the team boss with believing in the potential of young players like him who had been waiting for this opportunity.

Some said that in making a dream come true for academy graduates like Tammy, Frank Lampard had unlocked a level of passion and commitment that was sometimes lacking when buying in players on the transfer market. The young striker had grown up with Chelsea in his blood. His sole ambition as he rose through the ranks was to play for the senior team one day, and now that opportunity had arrived. All Tammy wanted to do now was make every moment count.

In bringing in players like Tammy, Callum, Mason, Ruben and Fikayo, Frank had silenced critics who claimed the academy made false promises. Now, players as young as eight who trained at the Cobham grounds looked at strikers such as Tammy and knew that with the same passion and commitment they could follow in his footsteps.

Season Goals

Tammy's talent was really starting to shine during the 2019–20 season. His goal in the team's 2–1 victory against his old club, Aston Villa, took his season's Premiership scoring total to twelve. It was an incredible number, especially for such a young player. It meant he was now chasing Leicester's Jamie Vardy for the top spot. Teammates like N'Golo Kanté even began challenging him to keep on scoring at every match. Some players might have caved under the pressure, but Tammy simply thrived on it, even though his reputation as a goalscorer meant that defenders marked him heavily. It meant he had to fight for space on the pitch and seize every opportunity, which he did with heart and soul.

By the end of 2019, Tammy had scored again in Chelsea's 2–1 Champions League win against Lille, which put the team through to the last sixteen, as well as in their 2–1 victory against Arsenal in the Premiership. As the season moved into 2020, it was clear the young striker was on a charge. With his club riding high in the Premiership, and a likely place in England's UEFA Euro Cup bid, Tammy could look forward to making his mark on the year as a homegrown player that the world would soon be watching.

TAMMY LEADS
THE WAY

Tammy Abraham has come far from that little boy with big ambitions. Back then, knocking a ball about in the park with his brother and their friends, he could only dream of playing for a Premiership team as well as his country.

Now Tammy has made that happen. It's taken years of hard work in training and on loan, and he made sacrifices when growing up to make the most of his playing time, opting to stay home and study rather than hang out with friends. With support from his family, as well as his academy coaches, Tammy has stayed true to his belief that one day he would make it. Even when academy critics flagged up that very few young players ever reached the senior team, Tammy didn't give up, and finally the club gave him that all-important break. It might have been forced by a transfer ban, but Tammy's success has encouraged The Blues to consider younger academy hopefuls.

In stepping out with his beloved Chelsea, Tammy Abraham has shown every kid who idolizes him that becoming a professional footballer is possible. While his story has only just begun, and a shining career awaits him, perhaps Tammy's greatest contribution to the world of football is the fact that young players now have a hero who started out just like them.

Tammy Abraham Timeline

2 October 1997   Tammy Abraham is born in Camberwell, South London.

2004   Tammy joins Chelsea's Academy training programme.

August 2013   Tammy makes his debut in Chelsea's Under-16 team in the first weekend of the 2013–14 season. One week later, he scores his first goal for the Under-19 side in a 2–1 win over West Ham.

28 March 2015   Tammy scores his first goal for England's Under-18 side in a 6–1 victory over Switzerland.

2015–16	Tammy is part of the Chelsea Youth Team that wins both the UEFA Youth League and the FA Youth Cup two years in a row.
April 2016	Chelsea's temporary manager, Guus Hiddink, arranges for Tammy to train with the senior team.
11 May 2016	Tammy is brought on as a substitute in his first Premier League match for Chelsea versus Liverpool. The game results in a 1–1 draw.
15 May 2016	One week later, Tammy makes his debut for Chelsea versus Leicester City in front of a home crowd at Stamford Bridge. The match ends in another 1–1 draw.
July 2016	Tammy is named in the squad for the England Under-19 European Championship campaign. The team reach the semi-final.

August 2016	Tammy signs on loan for one season to Championship team Bristol City.
September 2016	Tammy is selected to play for England's Under-21 side in the UEFA Under-21 European Championship. The team make it through the group stages that year, but go out in the 2017 semi-final against Germany.
May 2017	Tammy ends the season having scored twenty-three goals for the team, making him the joint second highest goalscorer in the 2016–17 Championship.
July 2017	Tammy joins Premier League team Swansea City for a season-long loan.
November 2017	Tammy is called up to play for England in two friendly matches versus Germany and Brazil.

May 2018	Tammy's loan to Swansea comes to an end. He scored eight goals in thirty-nine appearances, but the team struggled all season and are relegated from the Premier League.
May 2018	Tammy represents England's Under-20 side in the Toulon Tournament. The team win the title for the third year running.
August 2018	Tammy heads out on loan again, joining Championship side Aston Villa.
May 2019	Tammy ends the season with twenty-six goals in forty appearances, making him the second highest scorer in the Championship. Aston Villa are promoted to the Premier League.
August 2019	Tammy returns to Chelsea to play for the senior team. He is given the number 9 shirt, previously worn by legends Jimmy Floyd Hasselbaink and Fernando Torres.

14 August 2019	Tammy becomes the youngest player to score a hat-trick for Chelsea in a 5–2 victory over Wolverhampton Wanderers.
11 October 2019	Tammy makes his first competitive appearance for England in a UEFA Euro 2020 qualifier against the Czech Republic.
14 November 2019	Tammy scores his first goal for England in their 7–0 win over Montenegro. The victory secures their place in the UEFA Euro 2020.
March 2020	In an agreement between the Football Association, the English Football League, the FA Women's Super League and the FA Women's Championship, play in the Premier League and international games is suspended mid-season due to the coronavirus pandemic.

17 June 2020	Premier League football resumes, resulting in a 3–0 win for Manchester City against Arsenal and a 0–0 draw between Aston Villa and Sheffield United.
26 June 2020	Liverpool are crowned Premier League winners after a 30-year wait.

Tammy's Clubs

Chelsea

Club name: Chelsea Football Club
Nickname: The Blues
Founded: 1905
Current manager: Frank Lampard
Current league: Premier League
Crest: A ceremonial lion holding a staff

Bristol City

Club name: Bristol City Football Club
Nickname: The Robins
Founded: 1894
Current manager: Lee Johnson

Current league: Championship

Crest: A robin alongside the club's founding year

Swansea

Club name: Swansea City Association Football Club

Nickname: The Swans

Founded: 1912

Current manager: Steve Cooper

Current league: Championship

Crest: A swan in black and white

Aston Villa

Club name: Aston Villa Football Club

Nickname: The Villans

Founded: 1874

Current manager: Dean Smith

Current league: Premier League

Crest: A yellow heraldic lion against the team colour background (claret and sky blue)

Top Tammy Goals

Bristol City v Burton Albion, 13 August 2016

How it happened: five minutes into extra time, in what would be almost the last kick of the match, Tammy connected with a cross from Ivory Coast national Kodjia. With the ball in the back of the net, Tammy's goal resulted in a 2–1 victory over Burton.

First Goal in the Premier League

Crystal Palace v Swansea City, 26 August 2017
How it happened: towards the end of the first half, Tammy was first on the scoresheet, catching Leroy Fer's cross with his right foot and slipping it past the keeper.

First Goal for England

England v Montenegro, 14 November 2019
How it happened: the last to score in a 7–0 wipeout against Montenegro at Wembley, Tammy pounced when his childhood friend Sancho delivered the ball to his feet in front of a flailing keeper.

Arsenal v Chelsea, 29 December 2019

How it happened: in a hard-fought London derby, with Arsenal and Chelsea level with one goal each, Tammy collected a pass from Willian Borges da Silva, switched around and drilled the ball into the net. The late, eighty-seventh-minute goal would take Chelsea to a 2–1 victory against their old rivals.

What Can Tammy Teach Me About Goalscoring?

Playing Style

Tammy plays up front as a striker. He's on the frontline facing the defending players and the goalkeeper.

His role is to join or set up an attack, often receiving the ball and then turning to carve out a space behind the opposition.

Tammy's height gives him an advantage in the air. He's a physically confident player that allows him to challenge for high balls.

Signature Move

Tammy is famed for his ability to react fast.

He often collects a pass and hustles it around opposing players as they put in a tackle or block.

Creating a space by moving quickly, Tammy can scramble the ball into a shot for goal that always stretches the keeper.

He also has a feared reputation among keepers for converting crosses into goals with one or two touches, often from within the penalty area. It gives little time for the defence or the keeper to react.

Tammy likes to find the corner of the net. He often twists his body around an early shot to create an angle the opposition aren't expecting.

Team Tactics

Under Frank Lampard at Chelsea, Tammy has benefited from strong attacking support from both the wings and midfield. This means the ball can be fed to him up front from different directions.

Tammy has a flair for converting passes into shots at goal from unpredictable angles.

Tammy can rely on strong runs into the box from teammates such as Mason Mount and Callum Hudson-Odoi. This allows him to come alive close to goal and use his extraordinary ability to create space to shoot despite heavy marking.

Tammy's ability to receive a fast ball, contain it and shoot from close range with explosive power will continue to test defences for many seasons to come.

Tammy's Heroes

Tammy has always been keen to learn from other top strikers. He often goes on YouTube in search of finishing moves that inspire him. Here are the players who have been a big influence:

Cristiano Ronaldo

Position: Striker

Clubs: Manchester United, Real Madrid, Juventus

Career highlight: In the 2017 Champions League, Ronaldo scored ten goals for Real Madrid in the finals. The Portuguese star claimed five against Bayern Munich and three against Atlético Madrid and another two in the final against Juventus.

Spectacular stat: In 2009, Ronaldo was considered one of the best players in the world. He was snapped up by Juventus from Manchester United for a world record fee of £80 million.

Sergio Agüero

Position: Striker

Clubs: Independiente, Atlético Madrid, Manchester City

Career highlight: Agüero won the Golden Boot Award as top goalscorer in the 2014–15 Premier League, netting twenty-six goals for Manchester City.

Spectacular stat: The grandfather of Sergio's son is one of the most famous living footballers in the world, former Argentine star Diego Maradona.

Thierry Henry

Position: Striker

Clubs: Monaco, Juventus, Arsenal, Barcelona

Career highlight: In 2005, Henry netted his 186th goal for Arsenal and became the club's all-time highest goalscorer. In 2010, he claimed the record playing for France with a stunning fifty-one goals to his name.

Spectacular stat: A bronze statue of the phenomenal Frenchman stands outside Arsenal's Emirates Stadium, marking the club's 125th anniversary in 2011.

FOOTBALL LEGENDS

HARRY KANE

Be inspired by Football Legend, **Harry Kane**!

Discover the inspirational story of this top
player's journey from his early life in London
following in the footsteps of David Beckham
at school to his successes with Tottenham's
youth team and dream role as
England captain.

Packed with footie facts and match stats plus
Harry's career highlights.

FOOTBALL
LEGENDS

HARRY KANE

Emily Hibbs

KANE'S
FIRST KICKS

Harry Edward Kane was born on 28 July 1993 at Whipps Cross Hospital, London, just five miles down the road from White Hart Lane, Tottenham Hotspur's home stadium. Harry's mum, Kim, was an assistant at a dental practice and his dad, Pat, owned a garage. Kim and Pat were loving and supportive, and Harry's big brother, Charlie, was his best friend growing up. The Kanes were a family of football fanatics and huge Spurs fans.

Almost as soon as he could walk, Harry was toddling down to the local park with Pat and Charlie for a kickabout. The small playing field wasn't exactly a world-class stadium. There were no nets or markings, and certainly no cheering crowds, but the trio made do with a patch of grass and a couple of trees for goalposts.

Harry quickly became as obsessed with football as the rest of his family, and a highlight of the week was going to see Spurs play at White Hart Lane. At his first match, four-year-old Harry sat in the crowd, proudly wearing his white-and-blue Spurs shirt, spellbound by the incredible players racing around the field below him. His favourite player, striker Teddy Sheringham, had just transferred to Manchester United. But as one of Tottenham's all-time highest goalscorers he was still Harry's hero, and his preferred footballer to copy at the park. After watching a match, Harry and Charlie practised the tricky tackles and skilful finishes they'd seen at the Lane.

A Sporting Start

When Harry was six the family moved to nearby Chingford, hometown of another legendary footballer, David Beckham. Harry dreamed of following in David's footsteps and becoming a sporting star himself, so when he spotted an advert for a trial at Ridgeway Rovers, the local club that David played for when he was a boy, Harry knew he had to go for it.

At the warm-up, the coach of Ridgeway Rovers, Dave Bricknell, introduced himself to the ten boys hoping to join his team and asked if anyone was up for having a go in goal. Harry preferred scoring goals to saving them, but he was keen to show the coach that he was happy to do anything, so he put his hand in the air to volunteer. Harry played well as a goalkeeper, making some skilful saves, and Dave was impressed. But then someone suggested that he should try Harry on the pitch – it turned out he was even better on the field than he was between the posts. Harry ran around the training ground, scoring goals from way down the field.

The trials were a success. Every week, Kim or Pat drove Harry to the nearby training ground, where he worked on improving his technique and building up his strength. He soon became Ridgeway Rovers' number-one striker.

Rubbing Shoulders with Rivals

Ridgeway Rovers had lots of strong players. Scouts from bigger clubs often came to watch their matches. Less than a year after Harry had joined the team, a scout invited him to a trial session for the youth academy of a Premier League club – it wasn't Harry's beloved Spurs, but their rivals, Arsenal! Still, the opportunity to play for such a strong team was too good to miss. Compared to Ridgeway Rovers' training ground, Arsenal's facilities were state-of-the art, with pristine pitches, gyms and meeting rooms.

Academy Trials

Big clubs like Arsenal and Tottenham Hotspur do not offer open trials. Instead, the clubs send out scouts, people whose job it is to search for talented players from local teams. Once a scout has spotted a player they think the club might be interested in, they make a recommendation, and the academy coaches might invite that player to a trial. At the trials, coaches look for players that can fill gaps in their current line-up, as well as someone with a strong technique and a personality that will fit in with the team.

Harry performed well at the trials and signed up with Arsenal for a whole season. He made the most of every opportunity, and though he wasn't as fast as some of the other boys, his powerful shots often found their mark. At the end of the season, however, there was bad news. On a walk to the park together, Pat put a hand on Harry's shoulder. "I've got to tell you something," he said. "Arsenal have released you." It meant that he wouldn't be continuing at the club. The coaches didn't think he was athletic enough and were worried about his pace.

Harry was disappointed. He'd done his best for the academy, even though his heart belonged to another club, and they had still decided to let him go.

But Pat wasn't fazed, he told Harry that if they worked hard, he'd be chosen to play for another club soon enough.

Embarrassing Photo

Years later, when Harry was playing for Tottenham, Arsenal fans found an old photo of him wearing the Gunners' kit at the academy and shared it on the internet. They thought the photo proved Harry wasn't a true Spurs fan. But Harry hit back at his critics, saying, "I wanted to wear a Tottenham kit but I don't think that would've gone down too well. I was eight years old … I just wanted to play football."

FOOTBALL LEGENDS

RAHEEM STERLING

Be inspired by Football Legend,
Raheem Sterling!

Discover the inspirational story of this young
player's journey from his early life in Jamaica
to life as a young immigrant in North West
London, where his incredible football talent
put him on the road to superstardom.

Packed with footie facts and match stats plus
Raheem's career highlights.

FOOTBALL LEGENDS

RAHEEM STERLING

Musa
Okwonga

KINGSTON, JAMAICA, 1996

Raheem was just two years old, and he had only one parent left.

At the time his dad died, Raheem and his family were living in Kingston, the capital of Jamaica, in an area called Maverley. He was born there, six years after his sister, and it was the kind of place where everyone knew everyone, and where the children always played outside. When there was a storm, the rain would decorate the grey streets, and the children would rush laughing through the puddles; and because the rain was so warm, running in it felt like taking a shower.

People in Raheem's neighbourhood didn't have very much. They had to work hard just so there was enough for everyone. All they really had was their friends and their siblings and their mums and their dads, and some of them didn't even have that.

No one knew exactly what happened to Raheem's dad, but what they did know was that one day some people got very angry with him and went looking for him with their guns. When they found him, they didn't talk, they fired, and that's how they took Raheem's dad away.

It was one of the hardest times in Raheem's life, and it was about to get even harder. Soon his mum had to leave too. She couldn't find a job that paid well enough in Jamaica, so she went to the UK to study there and hopefully earn enough to support her children. Raheem was too young to understand why she had to go. All he knew was that he used to have two parents, and now it felt like he had none.

Surrounded By Love

But even though he had lost his dad forever and his mum had gone far away, Raheem was still surrounded by love. He and his sister went to live with their grandmother.

If he was good Raheem's grandmother would let him go and buy ice cream from the local shop. So many small towns in Jamaica have a shop like that, where it feels like you can buy anything. You normally find them on the corner of a street, and they look very small from the outside, but once you walk inside it's like being in a cave. You just have to tell the shopkeeper what you want, and he'll disappear into a little room at the back for a few seconds before coming out with whatever you asked for. You could ask him for some batteries, a toothbrush, a kettle, even a chicken – just give him a few minutes, and he would return with it in his hands.

That was how Raheem's life started: with some very sad times, but some very happy ones too. Ice cream, running through the rain – and, of course, lots of busy days playing football with his friends. But for him to have a life more exciting than he could imagine, he would have to get on a plane.

Coming soon!

Kick off your collection with more
Football Legends.

**Lionel Messi and Kylian Mbappé
available September 2021**